# From Daisy to Paisley

## 50 Beginner Free Motion Quilting Designs

By Leah Day

www.DayStyleDesigns.com

Publisher: Leah Day
Editors: Josh Day and Chet Day
Published by Day Style Designs, P.O Box 386, Earl, NC 28152

Email: support@daystyledesigns.com

www.daystyledesigns.com

Attention quilters, artists, and other crafters: Please feel free to use the designs in this book in your quilts, artwork, craft projects, etc. These designs were created to be used and shared to make the world a more beautiful place.

Attention teachers: This book is an excellent resource for teaching free motion quilting. Please go to www.DayStyleDesigns.com for more information about the Day Style Designs teaching program.

We have taken great care to ensure that the information included in this book is accurate and presented in good faith, but no warranty is provided nor results guaranteed. Having no control over the choices of materials or procedures used, neither the author nor Day Style Designs shall have any liability to any person or entity with respect to any loss or damage caused directly or indirectly by the information contained in this book.

Any similarities to existing designs, graphics, or patterns is purely coincidental.

From Daisy to Paisley contains 50 continuous line free motion quilting designs originally published on the Free Motion Quilting Project at:
**www.FreeMotionProject.com**

Library of Congress Control Number: 2010936284

ISBN: 978-0-9829930-2-6

# TABLE OF CONTENTS

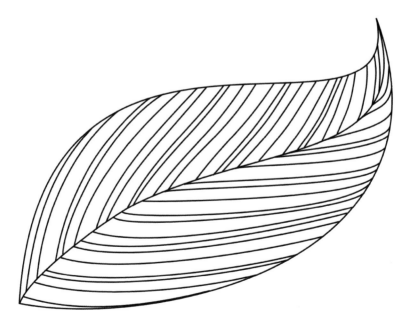

# THE FREE MOTION QUILTING PROJECT

In 2009, I challenged myself to create 365 new quilting designs and share them online at: FreeMotionQuilting.blogspot.com

There was only one rule: all of the designs had to be fillers.

**Filler designs are special continuous line designs that are quilted in free motion without marking or breaking thread.**

The idea for this project came to me while I was quilting this huge quilt with only two designs:

**Stippling** - The most popular and widely used filler design (pg. 14).

**McTavishing** - A wonderful design created by Karen McTavish.

After quilting half of the quilt, I started wanting more designs. So I came up with one of my own called **Flame Stitch** (pg. 30).

Creating this design was so easy, I quickly realized the potential for inventing new designs was endless! I set myself the task to come up with 365 new designs and share them all online with quilters from all over the world.

I hope you will enjoy the 50 beginner level designs featured in this book and have fun using many of them in your future quilts.

So without further ado... *Let's go quilt!*

Leah Day

# Filler Design Theory

A few months in to the project, I noticed that some designs didn't work very well in certain areas of my quilts.

Some designs work great in the sashing, open blocks, or plain borders of a quilt, while other designs work best in complex areas like around these appliqué flowers:

So what is it that determines where a design will work the best?

### It's the way a design is stitched that determines where that design will work best in your quilts.

Read through the design description at the beginning of each section to learn where that set of designs will work the best.

The wonderful thing about Filler Design Theory is that once you master one design, the rest of the designs in that section should come easily to you because they're all stitched in similar ways.

# ECHOING AND TRAVEL STITCHING

There are two fundamental techniques to free motion quilting that will be touched on throughout this book.

The first is **Echo quilting**:

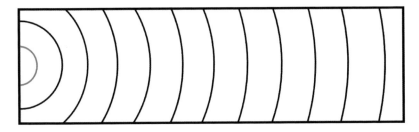

To echo, you will start with an initial shape (the green half circle) and then stitch around it a set distance away.

You can also think of echoing as parallel quilting because the echo line is stitched parallel to the line before it.

The starting shape can be anything at all. You can echo a shape on a block, an appliqué motif, or even a stitched line.

Echoes draw attention to your starting shape, create movement, and expand a design to cover more space on your quilt.

**The key to echoing is maintaining a set distance away from your starting shape.**

Your goal is to stitch a consistent distance away from your shape, otherwise your echoes could end up looking like this sloppy heart!

Another technique that must be mastered in free motion quilting is **travel stitching.**

Traveling is the process of stitching right on top of your previous stitching. We use traveling to get from one area of a quilting design to another, hence the name traveling!

By stitching right on top of the previous stitching you will be able to avoid breaking thread and keep the design flowing continuously.

Traveling also adds extra depth to any quilting design. The layers of traveled threads draw more attention to the quilting design and texture on the surface of your quilt.

**The most important key to traveling is staying right on top of the line you're stitching on.**

In the drawing on the right you can see correct traveling in Line A. Avoid stitching off the line as shown in Line B.

**A**        **B**

Some designs depend entirely on traveling. This drawing of **Fern & Stem** (pg. 70) is stitched by first creating the stem, then traveling along the stem to branch out with the curving leaves.

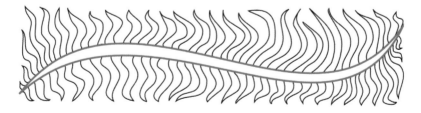

Try tracing this design starting with the green stem first. Then travel back over the stem and branch out with the leaf shapes. By traveling back over the stem you've already stitched, you can avoid breaking thread between every leaf.

# A NOTE ABOUT SCALE

All of the designs in this book can be stitched on any scale.

This means that you can stitch each design very small so it will fit into the tiny, complex areas of your quilt.

For example, this is **Lollipop Chain** (pg. 18) drawn on a ¼" scale:

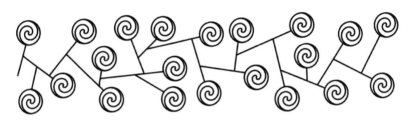

But you can also stitch each design on a large scale so it covers wide expanses of your quilt with every pass.

Here is the same **Lollipop Chain** design drawn on a ½" scale:

The photos within this book have been stitched on a ¼" scale to make viewing the textures easy, but all of the designs can easily be stitched much bigger in order to finish your quilts in less time.

# QUILTING ON A HOME SEWING MACHINE

There seems to be a prevailing notion that free motion quilting is impossible on a normal, home sewing machine.

**The truth is, with patience, practice, and the right tools, you can quilt all of the designs in this book on your regular machine!**

Remember back to the days you were just learning how to piece and appliqué. Chances are your first attempts weren't perfect.

But because you really wanted to learn how to make beautiful quilts, you stuck with it, took a few classes, read several books, and invested in special tools, like rotary cutters and rulers, to make the process easier.

Unfortunately, when most quilters get started free motion quilting, they expect perfect stitches from the very beginning.

Many forget that there is a learning curve to free motion quilting, just like there is for piecing or appliqué.

**This has caused many quilters to fear free motion quilting, or assume that this is just not possible on a domestic machine.**

But it absolutely is possible! If you approach free motion quilting with the same determination and enthusiasm as piecing or appliqué, you can definitely learn to free motion quilt.

# Tips on learning how to free motion quilt on your domestic sewing machine:

**1. Don't drop your feed dogs** - Not all machines are designed to work well with the feed dogs down, and it can greatly improve your stitch quality and tension to leave them up.

**2. Turn Your Stitch Length to 0** - Since your feed dogs may still touch the back of your quilt, turn your stitch length to 0 so the teeth will not actually feed your quilt forward.

**3. Invest in the right tools** - Every technique has a set of tools that make the process easier. Here's a list of tools that are absolutely essential for free motion quilting:

- **Supreme Slider** - This is a slick Teflon covered sheet that sits on the surface of your machine and reduces the friction between the back of your quilt and the table top. This makes the quilt much easier to move around - almost like it's gliding on air!

- **Little Genie Magic Bobbin Washers** - These are tiny Teflon washers that go inside your bobbin case and help your bobbin to glide more easily. This results in fewer thread breaks, better stitch quality, and fewer bird nests of thread on the back of your quilt.

- **Machingers Quilting Gloves** - In order to move your quilt easily you need to get a good grip on the quilt top. These nylon gloves have rubberized tips, perfect for gripping the quilt so you have more control over the designs you create.

- **Open Toe Darning Foot** - Darning feet are designed to hover over the surface of your quilt, making it easy to move the quilt around. If you can't find an open toe foot for your machine, consider using a generic plastic foot and breaking it open for better visibility over your stitches.

All of these tools and supplies can be found at:

## www.DayStyleDesigns.com

Independent Designs are stitched exactly the way you sign your name in cursive writing:

These designs are all created with a leading line that forms the design independently, filling the space as big or small as you choose.

The key with Independent Designs is to remember the shapes you're stitching so the design is continually being formed as you move forward.

Think of it like knowing how you write your name. You never forget what letter is next so you always know what movements to make.

## Where Independent Designs Work Best

Independent Designs work wonderfully in all areas of your quilt.

They can easily bend around complex motifs and look great stitched in both large and small scales.

If you want to think of each design type like a family, then **Stippling** would be the mother of all Independent Designs, so let's learn that design first!

# STIPPLING

Stippling is one of the most popular free motion quilting designs and because it's the base of so many designs, it simply had to be included in this book!

To stitch Stippling, start by stitching curving "U" shapes. Once you're able to stitch these shapes consistently, the next step is to elongate them, and add a bend here, and a bend over there and suddenly you will have a very complex stippling texture.

The only rule is to **not cross your lines** of quilting. Thankfully this is one of the only designs with such a tricky rule!

# WANDERING CLOVER

Wandering clover is our next Independent Design with a slightly different rule. This time you **must** cross your quilting lines!

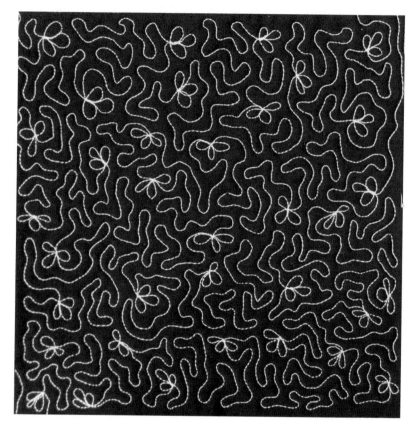

To stitch this design, you're first going to start with a short segment of Stippling. This is the "vine" that is chaining all of the clover leaves together.

To create a set of clover leaves, simply branch off with a set of 3 loops. Play with creating the loops in a variety of ways until you find a way that feels most natural to you. Continue to stipple and add a new clover patch wherever you like.

# PUMPKIN PATCH

Now let's bend the rules of Stippling again to create pumpkins:

This time you're going to stitch a wiggly, loopy vine that can cross and loop as many times as you like. Occasionally branch off this loopy line with a circle.

Fill the circles with curving lines, add a stem and leaf on the top, and what do you get? A pumpkin!

This design will still work in all areas of your quilt as long as you have enough space to fit a pumpkin shape in occasionally.

# FROG EGGS

Here's a design that proves how easy it is to combine designs. This design is created by combining **Stippling** (pg. 14) with **Pebbling** (pg. 37).

To stitch this design, simply wiggle your line around, filling the space evenly, then occasionally branch off with small clusters of circular shapes.

You can make the Pebbling clusters as big or small as you like, depending on how much you want them to stand out from the wiggly Stippling background.

# LOLLIPOP CHAIN

All of the Independent Designs we've learned have been based on curving lines. Let's see how this works with straight lines:

Lollipop Chain is created by first stitching a straight line, then stitching a circle.

Travel inside the circle and stitch an open spiral, leaving enough room for you to spiral back out of the circle.

Backtrack along your straight line about halfway down and then branch off with a new lollipop going in another direction.

# TEAR DROP TREE

Tear Drop Tree is another variation using straight lines, this time topping them with a single **Paisley** shape (pg. 21).

Tear Drop Tree is quilted by first stitching a straight line.

To stitch the leaves for this design, quilt a tear drop shape, then pivot off your starting point and echo the shape 2-4 times.

Both Tear Drop Tree and Lollipop Chain use **Traveling** (pg. 9), or stitching right on top of your previous stitching, in order to get from one area of the design to another.

Now it's time to learn a new design type that's very quick, easy to stitch, and creates an awesome, eye catching texture!

Pivoting Designs are easy to stitch and just like Stippling, they are all based off of one design: **Paisley!**

These designs are formed by stitching a shape, returning to your starting point, and pivoting off that starting point to stitch an echo around your design.

Try tracing this drawing starting on the red dot:

The design is formed by pivoting and echoing as many times as you like, then travel stitching along the edge of the design and branching out with a new shape in a different direction.

## **Where Pivoting Designs Work Best**

Pivoting Designs are terrific because they work wonderfully in all areas of your quilt, both big and small.

You can easily fit this design into tight spaces, or you can expand it and fill large areas of your quilt with every pass.

# PAISLEY

All Pivoting Designs are based on this simple tear drop shaped design called Paisley:

To stitch Paisley, first start with a single tear drop shape. Return to your starting point and echo the tear drop shape 2-5 times.

Travel stitch and branch off with a new tear drop and echoes in a slightly different direction.

Play with curving or straightening your initial tear drop shape for a slightly different effect in the finished design!

# POINTY PAISLEY

Creating variations of Paisley is very easy! This design works exactly the same, only this time you're using straight lines and sharp angles.

First stitch a triangle, then pivot off your starting point and echo that triangle 2-5 times.

The more echoes you stitch, the more your Paisley shape will stand out, and the more space it will take up! Have fun varying the number of echoes you use for each triangle to see what effects this can have on the texture of your quilts.

# DRUNK POINTY PAISLEY

Pointy Paisley is an awesome design, but what would happen if all the straight lines of the triangles suddenly became curvy?

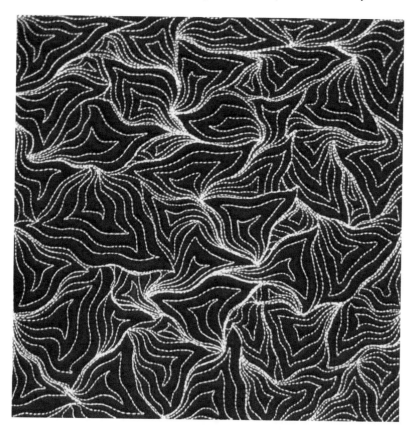

To stitch this design first stitch a wiggly triangle with two points, then come back to the starting point to create the third point.

Pivot off the starting point and echo the wiggly shape 2-5 times.

This design is very free-form and fun! Because you only have to think about creating two points, you have a lot more freedom to experiment with this design.

# MOON PAISLEY

You can use any shape as a base for these Pivoting Designs!
Let's see what happens when you use a crescent moon shape:

To stitch Moon Paisley, first stitch a gently curving crescent
moon shape and return to your starting point. Now pivot off
the starting point and echo the moon shape 2-5 times.

When you're ready to start a new crescent moon cluster, just
travel stitch along the edge of your last echo and branch off with
a new crescent moon shape in another direction.

# LOOPY PAISLEY

Remember the loopy line in **Pumpkin Patch** (pg. 16). Can this loopy line be made into a Pivoting Design? Of course!

To stitch Loopy Paisley, first stitch a single curving loop, then return to your starting point.

Pivot and echo your loopy shape 2-4 times, gradually branching out with bigger and bigger loops.

This fun design can be used in many ways! Check out **Loopy Flower** on page 73 for a fun variation of this simple design.

# PART 3

# ECHOING DESIGNS

Echoing Designs are created by first stitching a shape, then carefully echoing that shape many times.

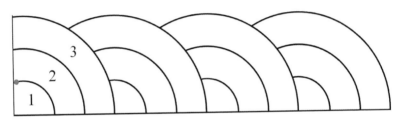

Try tracing this design starting with the red dot, and echoing each quarter circle down the row.

You might be wondering what the difference is between Echoing and Pivoting Designs. They certainly sound similar!

The difference is now you must **travel stitch** a distance away from the shape before echoing rather than just pivoting off the same starting point over and over.

**The size of your echo is determined by
how far you travel away from your initial shape.**

Due to the large amount of traveling involved with these designs, echoing designs are slightly more challenging, but with practice and patience you can definitely master this design type.

## Where Echoing Designs Work Best

You have ultimate control over how big your echoes are and how many times they surround each shape, so these designs will usually work very well in all areas of your quilt.

# ECHO SHELL

When I think of Echoing Designs, I usually think of Echo Shell, which is inspired by a traditional Baptist Fan design.

This version is much more free form because you can branch out with shells in all different directions:

To quilt Echo Shell, first stitch a half circle, travel stitch, and echo the half circle 2-5 times.

If you need to cover a lot of space quickly, start with a large half circle and travel stitch 1 inch to create large, space filling echoes.

# BRAIN CORAL

Variations of Echoing Designs are endless!  Let's combine a
**Stippling** shape (pg. 14) with echoing and see what happens:

First stitch a wiggly Stippling shape.  Travel stitch a set distance
away and echo that wiggly shape 3-5 times.

Continue to travel and echo the shape as many times as you like,
then branch out with a new wiggly shape in another direction.

This design has a very similar texture to Stippling, but because of
the echoes and traveling Brain Coral stands out a lot better!

# TRIPPY TRIANGLES

Not all free motion designs are soft and curvy. Let's learn how to echo using sharp angled triangles:

To quilt this design, first stitch a single triangle point and return to your starting line. Travel stitch along your starting line and echo the triangle a set distance away.

This example of Trippy Triangle was stitched using only one echo for each triangle shape. See how different the design looks with a set number of echoes rather than any number as with **Echo Shell** on page 27?

# FLAME STITCH

Are you looking for an Echoing Design with flowing movement and dynamic texture? Check out this fun design that starts with a flowing flame shape:

To stitch this design, start with a wiggly line, come to a point, and stitch back to your starting line. Travel stitch a short distance and echo the flame shape 3-5 times.

When you're finished with one flame, travel stitch and branch off with a new flame and echoes in a slightly different direction.

# Echo Hook

There's an amazing variety of textures you can achieve with Echoing Designs. The texture of this design is really just a combination of the shapes created in **Echo Shell** (pg. 27) and **Flame Stitch** (pg. 30):

To stitch this design, first stitch a curving, circular shape, but don't complete the circle all the way. Come to a point then echo this line back to the starting line to create your first hook.

Travel stitch and echo the hook 2-4 times. Travel along the last echo and branch off with a new hook in another direction.

# - PART 4 -

# FOUNDATIONAL DESIGNS

The last two design types we've learned were both based on a small starting shape. What would happen if our starting shapes were much bigger?

Foundational Designs are designs that start with a large base line that fills your whole quilting area.

In the diagram above, the foundational line starts at the red dot and bisects the whole quilting space with a curving line.

The rest of the open space is filled with echoes of this foundational line. One side has been left open so you can practice filling it in with echoes yourself.

## **Where Foundational Designs Work Best**

These designs can easily stretch across the whole surface of a quilt or within a specific area of a block.

Because you need to be able to evenly cover your quilting space with the foundation, this is going to be a design that works best in open, uncomplicated areas of your quilt.

This is also a design that will cover large spaces rapidly, so it's a great choice for a quilt you need to finish quickly!

# DESERT SAND

This is the first, most simplistic Foundational Design which starts with a freeform, gently curving line:

To quilt Desert Sand, first stitch a long, gently curving line. Come to a point and stitch off in another direction, keeping this line very open so you have plenty of room to fill later.

Once you've filled the entire area with a single, curving line, travel a short distance and echo this line multiple times until the entire space is filled on one side. Travel to the other side of the foundation line and fill the other side with echoes as well.

# JAGGED PLAIN

Variations of Foundation Designs are created as easily as changing your foundation line! This design starts with a foundation of straight lines and sharp angles:

To stitch this design, start by filling your quilting space with a very random jagged line. Try to keep your lines very straight and the angles sharp.

Once you've set the foundation, travel stitch and echo this foundation with more lines following the jagged path on both sides of the foundation.

# Ocean Current

The more complex a foundation you set, the more interesting your texture will be! Let's see what happens when we stitch a swirling, whirling foundation into our quilt:

To stitch Ocean Current, first set the foundation by stitching a large, open swirling line into your quilting space. Travel stitch and echo this line, stitching inside each swirl to make them stand out even more.

Once you've filled one side of your foundation with echoes, travel to the opposite side and fill it with echo lines as well.

# - PART 5 -
# STACKING DESIGNS

Now that we've learned about several types of echoing designs, let's move on to a set of designs created by stacking shapes on top of one another.

With Stacking Designs, shapes can be formed any size or shape, but to form the design, some area of the shapes must touch.

Joining shapes together can sometimes create a large amount of traveling in order to get from one area of the design to another.

These designs work a lot like a set of stacked bricks:

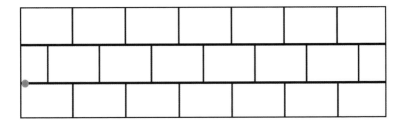

Try tracing just the bottom row of stacked bricks starting on the red dot and without lifting your pen! By not lifting your pen, you'll quickly see how much you must travel over your previous lines of stitching in order to create new stacked shapes.

## <u>Where Stacking Designs Work Best</u>

Because you can control the size and shape of the stacked design, these designs usually work in all areas of a quilt.

Also the extra thread built up in the traveled areas of the design will usually stand out beautifully anywhere on your quilt.

# Pebbling

The most well know and widely used Stacking Design is called Pebbling, and it's created by stacking circular shapes together.

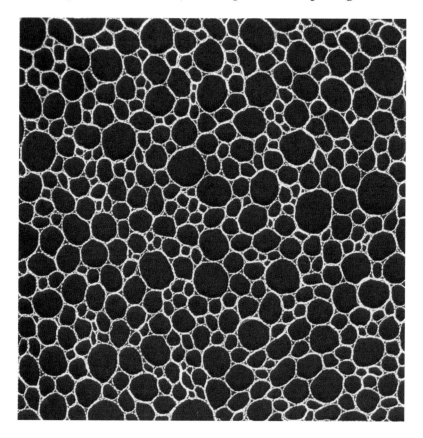

To quilt Pebbling, first start with a circular shape. It doesn't have to be a perfect circle because some pebbles are more oval than round.

Now stitch another circle, connecting the sides and stacking the two shapes together seamlessly.

Continue stacking pebbles, filling your quilt one circle at a time.

# COFFEE BEANS

Many shapes can be stacked together easily. Here's a stack of
ovals that become coffee beans with a simple curving line:

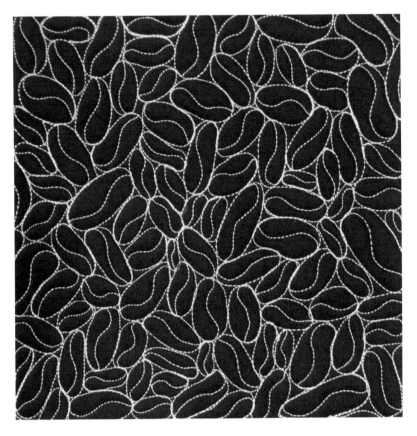

To stitch this design first start with a long oval shape, then stitch
through the oval with a gently curving line.

Stack another oval next to the starting oval, again filling it with a
curving line to create the appearance of a coffee bean.

Continue fitting more coffee beans together, travel stitching
where needed to move from one oval to another.

# BED OF ROSES

You can stack more than just circles and ovals! Here's a design created by stacking irregular flower shapes.

To quilt this design, first start with a wiggly, irregular circular shape. It might help to think of a cartoon rose.

Stitch inside the flower and with a small spiral. Travel stitch back along this line to return to the outside of the flower shape.

Finally, branch out with a new wiggly flower shape, stacking the two together so the sides touch, then fill it with a spiral as well.

# OIL SLICK

This design works almost exactly the same as Bed of Roses, only this time your spiral is wiggly too!

To stitch Oil Slick, first start with a large, wiggly circular shape.

Stitch inside this shape with a wiggly spiral, internally echoing the curves of the shape all the way to the center.

Travel stitch back along this spiral carefully to get out of the circular shape. Branch off with a new circular shape in a slightly different direction and fill it with a wiggly spiral as well.

We can create Stacking Designs with even the most basic shapes. Now let's stack some really simple squares and rectangles together to form this cityscape design:

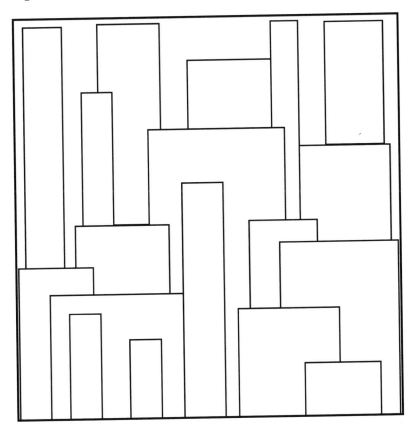

To quilt Cityscape, first stitch a row of simple squares and rectangles. To build up the levels of your city, travel stitch along the edges of the first row and add more squares and rectangles.

Interconnect each new shape so it appears as if some shapes are in front of others. This will work best in the open areas of your quilt where you have room to branch out with shapes of all sizes.

So far we've learned about a lot of designs that have very specific rules for how they are stitched.

But isn't it nice to occasionally break the rules?

Overlapping Designs definitely break all the rules - stitch anywhere you want and cross your lines as much as you like!

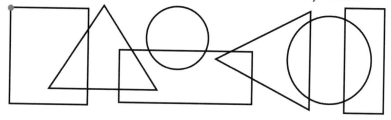

Overlapping Designs are exactly what they sound like - designs created by overlapping shapes to create complex textures.

Try tracing the overlapping shapes above starting on the red dot, and, once again, don't lift your pen!

By keeping your pen on the page the whole time, you'll be able to see how many times you will need to travel stitch to get from one shape to another without breaking your thread.

## **Where Overlapping Designs Work Best**

Overlapping Designs have a very complex texture that can easily get lost in the small areas of your quilt.

Therefore, this is a design type that will work best stitched really big, covering large areas of your quilt with graphic texture.

# Broken Glass

This Overlapping Design was inspired by comic books. When the super hero rushes in to save the day, shards of overlapping shapes fly through the air to create the illusion of broken glass.

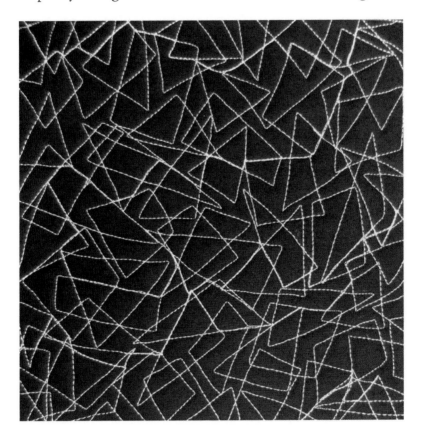

To stitch this design, first start with a triangle. Travel stitch along the edge and overlap the triangle with another triangle.

Feel free to experiment with shapes other than triangles.

The only rule with this design is your shapes must have straight lines and sharp angles. After all, broken glass is always sharp!

# Venn Diagram

You can overlap almost any shape or design. Now instead of straight lines and sharp angles, let's try overlapping circles:

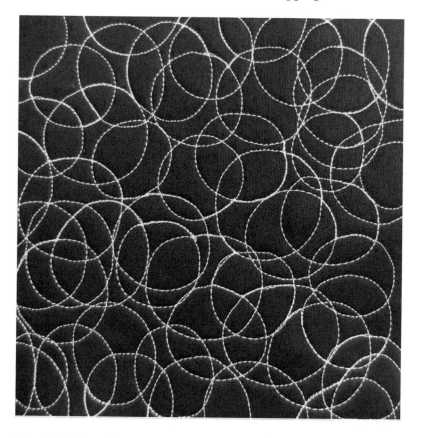

To stitch Venn Diagram, first start with a circle. Overlap this circle with a second circle, then branch out with a third circle, traveling along the edge so they're not all overlapping at the same point.

All of the circles in the picture above are about the same size. Play with stitching both big and small circles to see the way different sizes can affect the texture of this design.

# LOOSE WEAVE

Overlapping Designs can use more than just primary school shapes. Let's see what happens when we overlap curving lines:

To stitch Loose Weave, first stitch a long, gently curving line. Come to a point and echo back along this line, connecting the end together so it forms a long, skinny snake shape.

Travel stitch and overlap this shape with a new snake shape running perpendicular to the original line. Fill your whole space with horizontal and vertical overlapping snake shapes.

# - PART 7 -

# INTERLOCKING DESIGNS

Now let's learn about a new set of designs that literally locks together!

Interlocking Designs are created very similarly to Independent Designs, only now each new shape will dictate where the next shape is placed in the design.

The best example of an Interlocking Design is **Basic Spiral**. Each new spiral is formed interlocking with the spirals before it, but not touching the edges of any shapes.

Because the shapes don't touch, you must rely on visually gauging an area and filling it with a shape that will fit perfectly while still maintaining a consistent space between all the lines of quilting.

## Where Interlocking Designs Work Best

Interlocking Designs will work well in all areas of your quilt, both big and small. You have ultimate control over how big your shapes are and how easily they will fit together.

These designs are a bit tricky because you must gauge the size of the shapes to interlock them correctly. Try drawing each design to practice before quilting them on your quilts.

# BASIC SPIRAL

The mother of all Interlocking Designs is Basic Spiral because it perfectly illustrates how the shapes lock together without actually touching.

To stitch Basic Spiral, first start with an open spiral shape, leaving room for yourself to come to a point and then spiral back out of the design without travel stitching.

Immediately swirl into a new spiral, locking the designs together closely, but not touching. Move around your quilting space, forming spirals of all sizes so they lock together perfectly.

# SQUARE SPIRAL

It's no surprise that most Interlocking Designs are also spirals!
Here's an easy variation of Basic Spiral stitched with squares:

To stitch this design, first start with three sides of a square, then
spiral into this square, leaving room to stitch back out again.

To gauge the space you need to stitch out of a spiral, **double the
scale of your design** (pg. 10). For example, if you are stitching
on a ¼" scale, leave ½' open all the way into your square so that
on the way out you can stitch a line right through the middle of
the space you left open.

# ANGLE SPIRAL

Let's try another Interlocking Design only this time stitching any shape so long as it has straight lines and sharp angles.

To quilt Angle Spiral, first stitch a triangle or rectangle and spiral inside, again leaving plenty of space for you to get back out.

Branch off with a new open, angular shape, interlocking the two shapes together so they're close together, but not touching.

If you find yourself struggling to gauge how big your initial shapes should be, try drawing this design first to practice it.

# SHARP ANGLED MAZE

Can Interlocking Designs contain any travel stitching at all? Of course they can! Here's an easier variation of Angle Spiral stitched with closed spirals and lots of traveling:

To quilt this design, first stitch a triangle or rectangle and spiral inside, this time filling the space completely with your spiral.

When you get to the center of the spiral, stop and travel stitch back out of the shape, stitching right on top of the spiral line.

Now branch off with a new shape, interlocking it with the first.

# - PART 8 -
# EDGE TO EDGE DESIGNS

Now let's learn about a set of designs that are literally on edge!

These designs are created by stitching right across your quilting space from one edge to another.

With these designs, you must travel along the edges of your quilting space very often. Trace this design, traveling along the top or bottom edge to get to each new design line.

## Where Edge to Edge Designs Work Best

These designs work best when stitched in open areas of your quilt. Most Edge to Edge Designs are line based and it's very tricky to keep straight lines consistent in very complex areas.

These designs will work best in quilt sashing or border areas. They're also a great choice when you want to cover a quilt with one filler design, completely ignoring the pieced or appliquéd shapes you've created on the surface.

# MESH CURTAIN

Edge to Edge Designs are usually very simple to stitch, but the resulting texture can be so complex it's easy to get lost in it!

To quilt Mesh Curtain, stitch a curving line across your quilt space. On the opposite edge, travel stitch a short distance, then stitch back across the space with another curving line, overlapping the first line to form a interlocking braid (red lines).

Now travel along the edge and stitch another braid next to the first (green lines). Lock the two together with a third braid (blue lines), overlapping all the lines to create a mesh effect.

# FLOWING LINES

It's amazing just how many textures you can create with gently curving lines. Here's a design that uses organic, flowing lines and travel stitching to form a very unique texture:

To quilt this design, first start with a long, gently flowing line. Echo this line 1-3 times across your quilting space.

To form the gap areas, travel stitch along the last line you created, then branch off to create a small gap between the lines. Reconnect with your line and travel stitch to the opposite edge. Echo the last line 1-3 times before forming another gap line.

# BAMBOO FOREST

Very simple variations can create entirely new designs. See what happens when we combine horizontal and vertical curving lines:

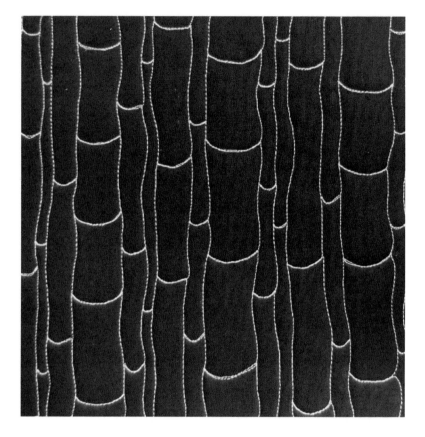

To quilt Bamboo Forest, first stitch a long, gently curving line across your quilting space.

Travel stitch and echo this first line, but stop occasionally and stitch a small horizontal curve to connect the two lines together.

You can expand or shrink the distance between your vertical lines to give the illusion of many different sizes of bamboo.

# FLAME KEY

This Edge to Edge Design was inspired by a Greek Key pattern, but is far simpler to quilt because all you have to do is echo!

To quilt Flame Key, first stitch a gently curving, zigzagging, flame shape from one edge of your quilting space to the other.

When you get to the opposite side, travel stitch and echo the first line perfectly, interlocking your flame key shapes.

Flame Key has a beautiful multi-directional texture because the lines flow both horizontally and vertically.

# RIVER PATH

**Echoing** (pg. 8) is an integral part of Edge to Edge Designs. Practice keeping your echoes consistent with this simple design:

To quilt River Path, first stitch a long "U" shape back and forth across your quilting space.

When you've filled your whole area with huge "U's", travel and echo the first line, filling one side of the space completely.

Travel stitch and echo the opposite side as well until the whole space is filled with evenly spaced echoes.

# Matrix Rays

Now let's try our hand at stitching straight lines in free motion!

To quilt Matrix Rays, first stitch evenly spaced straight lines from one edge of your quilting space to the other.

Next, stitch a gently curving line across all of the straight lines. Echo this line evenly so the distance between the curves stays the same throughout the design.

You can work Matrix Rays running horizontally and vertically across your quilt or diagonally as seen in the picture above.

# LEFT TURN, RIGHT TURN

What would happen if you stitched across your quilting space by simply taking a left turn then a right turn over and over?

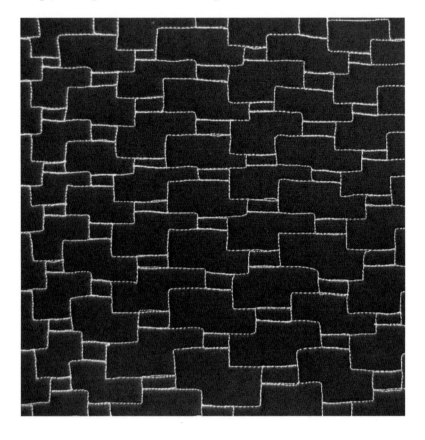

To quilt this design, first stitch a left turn, creating a 90° angle. Backtrack slightly then stitch a right turn, again creating a 90° angle. Backtrack again to get ready to stitch the next left turn.

Stitch across your whole quilting space this way. When you get to the opposite side, travel stitch and start a new row of turns, this time joining the left turns to the first row so the design creates an unbroken graphic texture across your quilt.

# ANGLE TURNS

Now let's create a simple variation of Left Turn Right Turn, only this time with narrow angles to create a sharper design:

To quilt Angle Turns, first stitch a left turn, creating a 35° angle. Backtrack slightly then stitch a right turn, again creating a 35° angle. Backtrack again to get ready to stitch the next left turn.

Stitch from one edge of your quilting space to the other simply by making these angular left turns and right turns. To start another row, travel stitch and interlock the left turns with the first row so the design forms a solid texture between the rows.

# MARIO VINE

Edge to Edge Designs really can be as simple or as complex as you like! Let's play with this basic design that combines straight lines with simple feather shapes:

To quilt Mario Vine, first stitch a straight line from one edge of your quilting space to the other. Travel stitch back along this line, branching out with simple feather shapes to either side.

To form the next row, travel along the edge of the quilting space to create the space between the rows, then stitch down to form the next straight line of the design.

# BUBBLE WAND

Combinations of simple shapes can create fantastic designs!
Bubble Wand is a simple mix of curvy lines and circles:

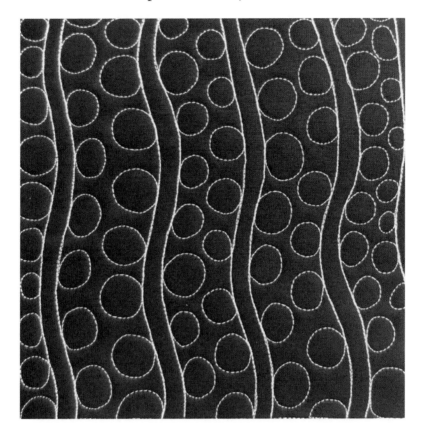

To quilt this design, first stitch a long, gently curving line across
your quilting space. Travel along this line, branching out with
circles along one side to form one half of the design.

When you get to the starting edge, travel stitch a short distance
and echo your first curvy line to form the second line.

Travel and again branch out with circles to complete the design.

# BASIC CHEVRON

Letters and numbers have inspired many new free motion quilting designs. This neat design is based off the letter "V."

**Note:** This design is tricky to line up properly. To simplify the process, you may want to mark registration lines on the surface of your quilt to indicate where the points should all match up.

Start with a "V" shape. Stitch a right angle to create space for your echo. Stitch a second right angle and echo the line, matching the points of the "V" shapes. Quilt from one edge of your quilt to the other, keeping all of the points lined up evenly.

In Part 8 we learned about designs that span the entire length of our quilting space. Now let's learn about designs that work from the edges into the center of your quilting space.

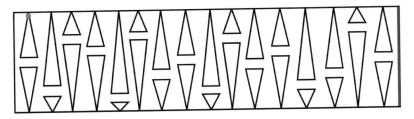

Again this set of designs utilizes the edges of your quilting space in order to move around the block to fill it completely.

Try tracing this design starting on the red dot traveling along the top edge to create each triangle. To get to the other side of the design, travel along the blue line on the side.

## Where Edge to Center Designs Work Best

These designs can be tricky to fit into tight or complex areas, so like Edge to Edge Designs, they work best in simple, open areas.

Sashing, borders, and open blocks are all great places to quilt Edge to Center Designs.

Sashing is an especially good choice because most of these designs are easy to stitch horizontally into sashing areas.

This is an area that most quilters leave blank, so definitely start looking at the sashing of your quilts to see where you can add a little extra texture with these free motion designs.

# WOBBLY COSMOS

Working from the edges of your quilting space into the center can create a gorgeous texture for your quilt. Can you believe this dynamic design is created with simple wiggly lines?

To quilt Wobbly Cosmos, first stitch a gently curving line into the center of your quilting space.

Now stitch back to the edge, gradually widening the distance between the lines of quilting as you move away from the center. Remember, there is more space on the edges than there is in the center, so the more space you take up on the edges, the better.

# Super Spiral

Now let's play with a simple variation of Wobbly Cosmos, this time stitching a giant spiral into the center of the quilt:

To quilt this design, first stitch a very open spiral into the center of your quilting space. Now stitch back to the edge, gradually widening the distance between the lines of quilting as you move away from the center.

Sometimes there just isn't enough space in the center for all the lines to fit. In this case, connect some lines to a previous line rather than into the center in order to keep the design consistent.

# Modern Art

Now let's experiment with an Edge to Center Design that runs horizontally along the edge of the quilting space.

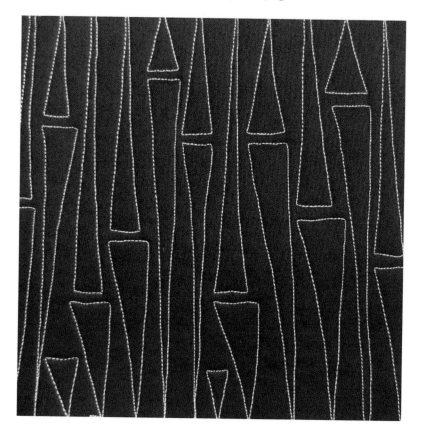

To quilt this design, first stitch a series of thin triangles in a variety of lengths into the center of your quilting space.

Travel stitch along the edge of the quilting space to the opposite side and stitch more triangles into the center, butting up against the triangles on the first side.

The resulting texture really looks like a set of jagged teeth!

# TRAILING SPIRALS

This design uses the same idea as Modern Art, except this time we're stitching open spirals instead of triangles!

To quilt Trailing Spirals, first stitch a long open spiral into the center of your quilting space and then echo back to the edge.

Stitch these spirals horizontally down your quilting space, varying the length and size of the spirals throughout.

Next travel stitch to the opposite side and stitch more spirals, interlocking them with the first set to form an even texture.

# Spiral Illusion

Just like Edge to Edge Designs, some Edge to Center Designs can appear so complex you can literally get lost in them!

To quilt Spiral Illusion, first stitch a square spiral into the center of your quilting space. When you get to the center, rotate your quilting space and stitch a new square spiral on top of the first, overlapping the lines until you get all the way back out.

It's very easy to get lost in the second spiral, so feel free to mark registration lines to make stitching the second half of the design much easier.

In Part 8 we learned two designs, **Mario Vine** (pg. 60) and **Bubble Wand** (pg. 61), that were worked from Edge to Edge but that also built off a central stem.

Now let's explore more Stem Centered Designs that can be quilted over your whole quilting space!

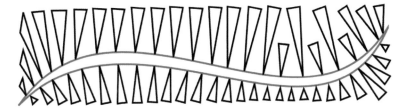

Stem Centered Designs always start with the center stem first, then the "leaves" are added by traveling along the stem.

Try tracing the drawing above starting with the green center stem, then branching out to create the triangle shaped leaves.

## Where Stem Centered Designs Work Best

Stem Centered Designs have a lot in common with Foundational Designs because the bulk of the design is first determined by your starting stem.

So these designs are going to work great in the open areas of your quilt where you have more than enough room for the stem and leaves to expand and fill the quilting space.

Try the following designs in a quilt where you're ignoring all the piecing lines in favor of an all-over, multi-directional texture.

# FERN & STEM

The easiest Stem Centered Design is created with simple curving lines that which add a gorgeous texture to the surface of your quilts.

To quilt this design, first stitch a gently curving line throughout your quilt. Echo this line ¼" to ½" away to form the stem.

Now travel along the stem and branch out with gently curving leaves. Feel free to experiment with varying the size and length of your leaves to take up more or less quilting space as needed.

# ELODEA

You can easily create new Stem Centered Designs by changing the leaf shapes. Here's what it looks like when you use triangles:

To quilt Elodea, first stitch a gently curving line throughout your quilt. Echo this line ¼" to ½" away to form the stem.

Now travel along the stem and branch out with thin triangles.

In the picture above, you can see how this texture builds up over the surface of the quilt when you stitch multiple lines of Elodea, interlocking all of the triangles together.

# LEAF VEINS

Within all design types there are designs that break the rules. Because of the way it's created, Leaf Veins will work better in smaller areas of your quilt, like inside appliquéd leaves (pg. 5).

To quilt Leaf Veins, first stitch a straight line. Travel along this line, branching out with long, curving lines all the way to the edges of your quilting space.

Travel along the edge and echo the last vein line to get back to the stem. Experiment with varying the space between the vein lines to see the effect this can have on your quilt.

# PART 11

# CENTER FILL DESIGNS

In Part 9 we explored Edge to Center Designs. Now let's see what happens when we do the opposite and work from the center of a space to the outside!

Center Filled Designs, like most free motion quilting designs, depend on traveling in order to move around the central circle to form the design.

Practice tracing this design starting in the center circle, then branch out with the simple petal shapes. Travel and echo each shape, moving continuously from the center to the outer edges.

## Where Center Fill Designs Work Best

Because you have to start in the center to create a Center Filled Design, these designs work best in the open areas of your quilt.

Open blocks, cornerstones, and even circular appliqué shapes are all great places for any of the designs in this section.

# STOMACH LINING

If you remember back to **Stippling** (pg. 14), we first started by creating wiggly "U" shapes. Now let's take those shapes and see what happens when we stitch them from the center of a block!

To quilt this design, first start in the center of your quilting space and stitch very small "u" shapes forming a spiral. As you spiral around, gradually expand your shapes and the distance between your lines of quilting.

By the time you get to the edges of your quilt, your shapes will be huge, making the tight center stitching stand out dramatically.

# LOOPY FLOWER

Of course, when you work from the center, you can start playing with many different flower shapes!

To stitch this design, first start with a small center circle. The petals of this design are created with **Loopy Paisley** (pg. 25).

Stitch a loop, return to your starting point, pivot and echo with as many loops as you like. Branch off with more petals evenly spaced around the center. Travel along the sides of the first petals to fill the background around the flower with more petals and curving lines.

# Super Daisy

A wonderful side benefit of Center Fill Designs is they appear harder to stitch than they really are! This daisy design looks complicated, but it's actually extremely easy to quilt.

To quilt Super Daisy, first stitch a small circle. Next stitch a set of small tear drop shaped petals off this center circle, spacing them evenly so they're all about the same size.

Now continue stitching around your daisy, echoing each petal shape. As you stitch around and around the center, gradually expand each petal to fill your quilting space completely.

# BEGINNER FREE MOTION QUILTING FILLERS DVD

Within this book you've learned how to quilt 50 beginner level designs, plus **Stippling, Paisley,** and **Pebbling**.

But sometimes a photo or drawing just isn't enough to get the hang of how a design is stitched in free motion!

This is why I've created **Beginner Free Motion Quilting Fillers**, a 2 hour DVD that features the following 30 designs from this book:

| | |
|---|---|
| Stomach Lining | Venn Diagram |
| Modern Art | Super Spiral |
| Mesh Curtain | Left Turn, Right Turn |
| Frog Eggs | Lollipop Chain |
| Flowing Lines | Matrix Rays |
| Bubble Wand | Angle Turns |
| Trailing Spirals | Basic Chevron |
| Wobbly Cosmos | Pumpkin Patch |
| Angle Spiral | Desert Sand |
| Bamboo Forest | Tear Drop Tree |
| Leaf Veins | Elodea |
| Square Spiral | Broken Glass |
| Mario Vine | River Path |
| Flame Key | Oil Slick |
| Super Daisy | Pointy Paisley |

**Beginner Free Motion Quilting Fillers DVD is available at:**

## www.DayStyleDesigns.com

# INDEX

Made in the USA
Lexington, KY
16 April 2014